snapshot•picture•library

EMERGENCY VEHICLES

snapshot·picture·library

EMERGENCY VEHICLES

FOG CITY PRESS

Published by Fog City Press,
a division of Weldon Owen Inc.
415 Jackson Street
San Francisco, CA 94111 USA
www.weldonowen.com

WELDON OWEN INC.
Group Publisher, Bonnier Publishing Group John Owen
Chief Executive Officer and President Terry Newell
Senior Vice President, International Sales Stuart Laurence
Vice President, Publisher Roger Shaw
Vice President, Creative Director Gaye Allen
Executive Editor Elizabeth Dougherty
Assistant Editor Sarah Gurman
Art Director William Mack
Production Director Chris Hemesath
Production Manager Michelle Duggan
Color Manager Teri Bell

A WELDON OWEN PRODUCTION
© 2008 Weldon Owen Inc.

Library of Congress Control Number: 2008935243

ISBN-13: 978-1-74089-997-0

10 9 8 7 6 5 4 3 2
2010   2011 2012

Printed by Tien Wah Press in Singapore.

We need help right away when there's an emergency. That's when ambulances, fire trucks, and police cars come to the rescue. Their flashing lights and loud sirens warn people that they are in a hurry.

But what happens when there's an emergency high in the mountains or far out at sea? The emergency services have it covered. Helicopters, sleds, and speedboats carry people back to safety. So, put on your seat belt and watch some amazing rescue vehicles in action.

When the fire
alarm rings, these
fire engines are
ready to go. Signals
inside the station
can even make
traffic lights turn
red to stop traffic.
Off they go!

Police cars and motorcycles are on the alert, too. In any kind of emergency, the police will be ready...

...and waiting for action! Police motorcycles travel quickly on busy city streets and highways. You can see motor units like these all over the world.

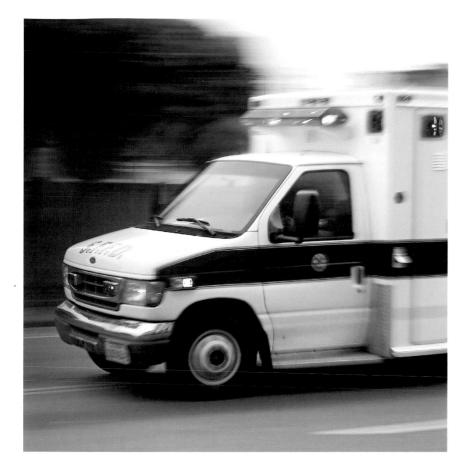

The word "ambulance" is written backwards so that people can read it in their rear-view mirrors!

Cars and people on crowded city streets can get in the way of rescue work. A line of police cars acts like a fence around the scene.

Rescue workers arrive with their equipment. A yellow pumper truck pumps water from a fire hydrant to hoses.

Each rescue
worker has a
specific job
to do—from
helping an
injured person,
to hosing down
the fire.

Police officers and firefighters must work together quickly and safely in an emergency.

Inside this ambulance is a stretcher for transporting an injured person to the hospital.

Helicopters can hover, or stay in one place, in the air. They can patrol the scene from the skies.

Air ambulances can land in difficult spots and quickly carry people away to safety.

This helicopter is lifting off with a patient on board. Paramedics in the ambulance responded first, but the helicopter can get to the hospital faster.

Sirens on! Ambulances rush injured people to the hospital. The blue symbol on some ambulances is called the "star of life."

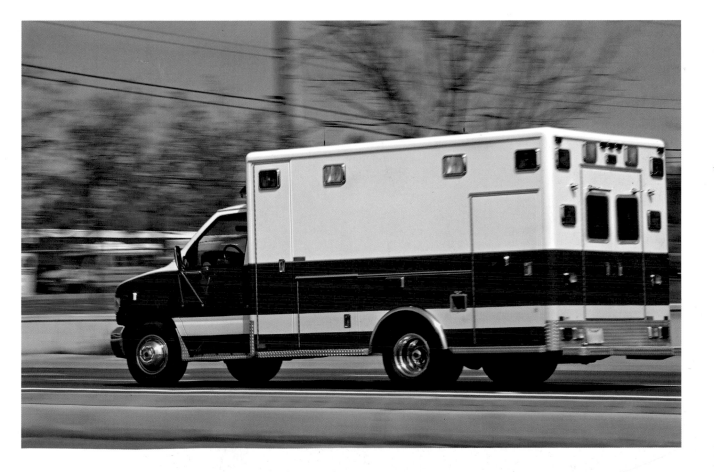

Water fights the flames. Hoses are hooked up to the hydrant and, whoosh! Out comes the water!

Special knobs
on the truck
control the
water power.
The inside of a
fire truck is like
a giant toolbox.

Fire-fighting
helicopters drop
water or foam
from tanks or
buckets onto
wildfires.

Airports have
fire engines
called "crash
tenders." Their
nozzles send out
jets of water or
foam to put out
airplane fires.

What about
when there's
a fire at sea?
Fireboats shoot
out water from
huge pumps
and nozzles.

The bright orange rescue boat is easy to spot from all around. Have you seen a life ring like this at the beach?

If you're in trouble in the water, a lifeguard can ride a personal watercraft to reach you.

Police and coast
guard crews
use boats to
rescue people
and to patrol
the waters.

This boat is fast and light. It stays strong and sturdy, even if lots of water splashes on board. A radio alerts the people waiting on shore.

Up above, coast guard helicopters hover over the sea and help anyone in trouble.

High in the
mountains,
helicopters
send rescuers
down by rope
and pull people
up again, too.

Helicopters can land on snow.
They're an option for mountain
rescues where there are no roads.

Snowmobiles, sleds, and all-terrain vehicles, can also come to the rescue in the snow.

This air ambulance
whizzes back to
the hospital. It
will land on the
hospital roof where
doctors are waiting.
A job well done!

Police motorcycle

Police motorcycles are small enough to weave through heavy traffic. They can also escort other emergency vehicles, such as fire trucks, to the scene.

Police car

A loud, flashing siren on top of a police car signals to drivers that they have to let the police through. The officers must get to where they're needed fast!

Police helicopter

Police helicopters can quickly bring people to and from an emergency situation. They fly up high and communicate with people on the ground by radio.

Paramedic ambulance

Ambulances with paramedics onboard race to where people need immediate medical help. They can transport injured or sick people to the hospital.

Fire truck

Fire trucks carry hoses to hook up to fire hydrants, which provide water to put out flames. The trucks also carry ladders, crowbars, wrenches, and ropes.

Crash tender

Crash tenders are fire trucks stationed at airports. Some have a "snozzle," a high-pressure nozzle for water or foam that can pierce an airplane to fight a fire inside.

Fire boat

These rescue boats fight fires at sea by pumping water and shooting it onto flames. They can also transport firefighters, police officers, and paramedics.

Fire-fighting helicopter

Fire-fighting helicopters spray wildfires with water or chemical retardant from above. They also transport fire crews, deliver equipment, and evacuate injured people.

Rescue helicopter

Coast guard rescue helicopters help people at sea and along the coast. They lower ropes to reach injured people and bring them safely onboard.

Rescue boat

Police rescue boats often patrol the sea to make sure everyone is safe. These boats carry life jackets and first-aid supplies, just in case someone needs help.

Personal watercraft

Often called Jet Skis after a popular brand name, personal watercraft allow rescuers to quickly reach people who are in trouble at sea, in a river, or on a lake.

Snowmobile

With skis in the front to steer and tracks in the back, snowmobiles can travel over snow and ice. They can be used for rescues on snowy days, even in the mountains.

ACKNOWLEDGMENTS

Weldon Owen would like to thank the staff at Toucan Books Ltd, London, for their assistance in the production of this book: Ellen Dupont, managing director; Cynthia O'Brien, author and researcher; Leah Germann, designer; and Hannah Bowen, project manager.